MARITAL RAPE:-A MYTH OR A SCANDALOUS REALITY?

VOLUME 2, ISSUE 1 OF BRILLOPEDIA

RISHIKA SALUJA AND MEGHA SINGH NARUKA

ISBN 979-888606542-8

Contents

Preface

"Start writing, no matter what. The water does not flow until the faucet is turned on".

-Louis L'Amour

Hundreds of students and professors are contributing their work to Brillopedia, we are here to provide ample information about Law and Contemporary issues. Our aim is to provide a platform for today's generation to express their views and ideas on law and contemporary law.

Publication

This research paper is published in volume 2, issue 1 of Brillopedia

Authors

Rishika Saluja

Megha Singh Naruka

ABSTRACT

India could be a country with diverse culture and values in its dimension. Marriage is one important ingredient that shows how our culture is structured. Marriage could be a bond between two individuals which eventually give them legitimacy for sexual issues.Violence against women isn't new our society, an area where a girl is anticipated to stay silent irrespective of how hard or how badly she is being treated. Here arises a matter that, whether the implied consent, given at the time of getting into that "contractual bond relationship" means the consent for everything that extends till the full period of life or has any limit when viewed within the aspect of ladies.Society has created this vague, imaginary idea of a perfect woman. One who listens to what people say, who obliges to each order, who remains quiet and suffers all types of agony mainly is physical, emotional, and mental.

Thus we are able to say that we board a misogynistic society and therefore the time is yet to come back where it's visiting to be an Egalitarian society i.e., a gender-neutral society.

"The murderer destroys the physical body of his victim. Rapists degrade the very soul of helpless females."

CHAPTER TWO

RAPE IN IPC

Rape, generally referred to as balatkar that is a terrifying word in itself. In India, it's one among the foremost common criminal activities. So petrifying, humiliating, traumatic and terrifying the word rape is that it destroys the whole psychology and effects the deepest emotions of the person being raped. The word rape has been derived from the Latin word 'rapio' which implies to take away. Therefore the literal meaning of rape might be forcibly snatching something from someone which is clearly an offence. To force means to indulge in an activity without the consent of another. Indian customs tend to believe in the concept of MaatriDevoBhava or treating women as goddess, which implies to worship women or mothers. But keeping in sight the quantity of rape cases which arise on a daily basis in India the concept of MaatriDevoBhava seems to disappear nowadays. Rape is a crime not only against the victim as an individual but against society as an entire. So utterly shameful is that the offence that it even is a crime against the fundamental human rights. No single definition can define the word rape attributable to its exhaustive nature. Only the one who suffers it, knows it. Therefore rape are often termed as a sexual abuse.

Rape is criminalized under Section 375 of I.P.C

Section 375 – Rape

"A man is said to commit "rape" if he:

1. Penetrates his penis, to any extent, into the vagina, mouth, urethra or anus of a woman or makes her do so with him or any other person; or

2. Inserts, to any extent, any object or a part of the body, not being the penis, into the vagina, the urethra or anus of a woman, or makes her do so with him or any other person; or

3. Manipulates any part of the body of a woman so as to cause penetration into the vagina, urethra, anus, or any of the body of such woman or makes her do so with him or any other person; or

4. Applies his mouth to the vagina, anus, urethra of a woman or makes her do so with him or any other person,

Under the circumstances falling under any of the following seven descriptions:—

First– Against her will.

Secondly– Without her consent

Thirdly—with her consent, when her consent has been obtained by putting her or any person in whom she is interested, in fear of death or of hurt.

Fourthly– with her consent, when the man knows that he is not her husband and that her consent is given because she believes that he is another man to whom she is or believes herself to be lawfully married.

Fifthly – With her consent when, at the time of giving such consent, by reason of unsoundness of mind or intoxication or the administration by him personally or through another of any stupefying or unwholesome substance, she is unable to understand the nature and consequences of that to which she gives consent.

Sixthly– with or without her consent, when she is under eighteen years of age.

Seventhly – when she is unable to communicate consent.

CHAPTER THREE

EXCEPTIONS OF SECTION 375 OF IPC ARE

Exception 1 – A medical procedure or intervention shall not constitute rape.

Exception 2– Sexual intercourse or sexual acts by a man with his wife, the wife not being under fifteen years of age, is not rape.

Here, according to exception 2 of section 375

"MARITAL RAPE IS NOT A CRIME IN INDIA" – Yes, Marital Rape is a type of Rape which is Legal in India.

"The husband can't be guilty of rape committed by himself upon his lawful wife, for by their mutual consent and contract upon his lawful wife hath given up herself this type unto her husband which she cannot retract".

MARITAL RAPE

"forcefulsexual acts committed without the consent of the partner." In layman language sexual intercourse with your own wife without her consent is **NOT**a crime in India. Though this nonconsensual sex between the spouses is considered as a criminal offence in many countries. However, India is one of the thirty six countries that still not have criminalized Marital Rape.

CHAPTER FIVE

TYPES OF MARITAL RAPE

Marital rape is also known as spousal rape or partner rape ,this is the type of rape which happens between the people who are known to be a wedded pair. There are three types of marital rapes which are identified by the legal scholars as generally pervasive in the society:-

1. BATTERING RAPE:-In battering rape ,women experience both physical and sexual violence and they experience this violence in different ways, some women are abused during the sexual violence and in some cases rape follows the physical asaultepisode where hte husband wants to make up and persuade his wife to hve sex against her will. The majority of marital rape victims fall under this category.

2. FORCE- ONLY RAPE:-In this type of rape man uses only the amount of force necessary to coerce his wife; battering may not be proclaimed in these relationships. These assault are transpires after the women refuses for sexual intercorse.

3. OBSESSIVE RAPE:-Some women also experience what has been labelle sadistic rape; these assaults involve torture and/or perverse sexual acts and are often physically violent.

Women are at particularly high risk for being raped by their partners under the following circumstances:

- Women married to domineering men who view them as 'property'
- Women who are in physically violent relationships
- Women who are pregnant
- Women who are ill or recovering from surgery
- Women who are separated or divorced

Approximately 10-14% of married women are raped by their husbands within the u. s..Approximately one third of girls report having 'unwanted sex' with their partner. Historically, most rape statutes read that rape was forced gender with a lady not your wife, thus granting husbands a license to rape. On July 5, 1993, marital rape became against the law all told 50 states, under a minimum of one section of the sexual offense codes. In 20 states, the District of Columbia, and on federal lands there aren't any exemptions from rape prosecution granted to husbands. However, in 30 states, there are still some exemptions given to husbands from rape prosecution. In most of those 30 states, a husband is exempt when he doesn't need to use force because his wife is most vulnerable (e.g., she is mentally or physically impaired, unconscious, asleep, etc.) and is unable to consent. Women who are raped by their husbands are likely to be raped many times—often 20 or more times. They experience not only vaginal rape, but also oral and anal rape. Researchers generally categorize marital rape into three types; force-only rape, battering rape and sadistic.

CHAPTER SIX

VIOLATION OF CONSTITUTIONAL RIGHTS

THE RAPE LAWS IN OUR COUNTRY DOES NOT CONSIDER MARITAL RAPE AS A CRIME – IT FEELS LIKE VIOLATION OF RIGHTS GIVEN IN THE CONSTITUTION.

· ARTICLE 14 &

· ARTICLE 21.

Article 14 of the Indian Constitution Specifies -"Equality before Law"- the state shall not deny to any person equality before the law or the equal protection of the laws within the territory of India.

Article 14 specifies equality before law and equal protection to everyone by law. But in this scenario (of Maital Rape) our law doesn't provide protection to married women's. In 1860 when I.P.C. was drafted at that time there was no independence for married women and till date these laws are not evolved till now also married women have no independent legal entity and are still treated as an entity within the husband's possession. In exception 2 of section 375 of the same act provides protection to the married girls under the age of 15 and not above 15. Thus, this exception clearly discriminates between married women who are below 15 and others who are above 15. Therefore, exception 2 of section 375 of the same act violates article 14 of the constitution.

Article 21 of the Indian Constitutionspecifies- "protection of life & personal liberty"- No person shall be deprived of his life or personal liberty except according to procedure established by law.

Article 21 of the constitution provides protection of life and personal liberty to all the citizens of India which also includes the right to privacy, dignity, health, safe environment, etc. In SuchitaSrivastava v. Chandigarh Administration judgement Supreme Court stated that Right to make choices in sexual activity is also included under the right to personal liberty which is a part of Article 21. The forced sexual intercourse by their husband spoils the wife's physical and mental health.

CHAPTER SEVEN

DOES MARRIAGE JUSTIFY RAPE?

On 26[th]August 2021 (Thursday) Chhattisgarh HC discharged a man from facing a trial for repeatedly raping his wife given the Indian law does not recognize marital rape as an offence. Justice N.K.Chandravanshi relied upon exception 2 of IPC section 375 which states that which states that "sexual intercourse or sexual act by a man with his own wife, the wife not being under fifteen years of age, is not rape." In this case justice N.K.Chandravanshi noted that, defendant had an intercourse with his legally wedded wife and hence passed a judgment stating that "SEXUAL INTERCOURSE BY A HUSBAND NOT RAPE; EVEN IF BY FORCE OR AGAINST HER WISH."

"Marital Rape is much more painful than rape because you have to get up with the tears & wipe it off with the same bed on which before you used to cuddle."

"Marital Rape exception takes away a married woman's ability to say 'JOYFUL YES' to sexual intercourse, that her sexual desire and consent is reduced to a nullity"- says Adv. KarunaNundy in a marital rape case

CHAPTER EIGHT

CONCLUSION

The Indian Government so as to safeguard women enacted/amended many laws as time passed. But it slows itself in enacting the laws against the horrible crime against the ladies by their own husband's referred to as marital rape. India till this era holds its position at the highest in protecting and practising its culture.

There is visiting be a continuing spike in cases with regards to Marital Rape and it's time the govt. both at the middle and state level recognizes this issue, the urgency, and necessity for laws to be enforced, enacted to guard the rights and dignity of a woman.

Though Indian culture holds the position of a better half under their husband's will, on the opposite hand, the identical said Indian culture also gives its voice in respecting the dignity of ladies and their consent all told necessary issues which involve them. Marriage not only involves men but also includes women on the opposite side to balance the ceremony"Marriage".

Women not only face health issue after this forceful unrealistic sex but they also undergoes many mental traumas like anxiety, depression, shock, fear suicidal ideation.

Thus, we are able to conclude that India recognizes marital rape as a criminal offense but it refuses itself to enact a correct law and to codify the crime.

"But the criminalization of Marital Rape in India is still a distant dream for all."